D1520344

The NFT Overview

A

Beginner's

Introduction to Digital

Currency, Art, and

Collectibles

Michael Maverick

Table of Contents

Introduction 1

Chapter 1: What Is an NFT? 5

The Short Answer 6
Fungibility and Value 9
A New Age of Digital Property 12

Chapter 2: Crypto & Ethereum 15

What is Cryptocurrency? 16
Why Crypto is Valuable 20
Ethereum and Smart Contracts 23

Chapter 3: The Market 29

Who Wants In? 29
Content Creators 31
Investment 32
Speculation 35

Chapter 4: Causes for Concern 39

Energy and Pollution 39
Bubbles 43
Legal Grey Area 46
Scams 53
Gas Fees 55

Chapter 5: Art and Music 59

Digital Rights of Artists 59

Safe Value 63

IP and Smart Contracts 64

Chapter 6: Sports and eSports 67

NFT's Origins 68

Rebirth of Sports Collectibles 71

Video Game Assets 74

Chapter 7: How to Get Involved 77

How to Buy and Trade 78

How to Make an NFT 81

How to Watch the Market 83

Chapter 8: The Future 87

Implications of the New Tech 87

Think of the Possibilities 91

Distributed IP Going Forward 96

Conclusion 100

References 102

Introduction

In 2021, a graphic artist calling himself Beeple sold a JPEG for $69 million. A JPEG is a common and ordinary digital image format. You see images using that format every day when you use the internet. In fact, you can find an exact copy of this particular piece of art, in a JPEG format, and download it right now. Just use your search engine and look up "Everydays — The First Five Thousand Days JPEG." When you find it, just download it and save it. You now have a piece of art for free that someone else paid more money for than most people earn in their entire lives.

If you are confused, don't worry. You are in good company. Most people are very confused by this. Before you are halfway through this book, you will not be confused anymore. You will know more about this topic than the majority of people on earth. By the time you are done with this book, you will probably be asking where you can buy a few hundred dollars in a share of Beeple's art, too.

Things happen slowly and then all at once. As you're reading all this and getting a sense of the direction things are going you might be understanding that this wasn't abrupt. It burst into the public consciousness because of a handful of very newsworthy sales that had most people scratching their heads and asking a lot of questions. Beeple is not a nobody in the art world. He's worked for Arianna Grande, SpaceX, and Nike. He may be new to you but he's not new to people in the know.

There is a massive explosion of activity into this new technology of digital ownership, energized by these major sales and the news coverage of them. Some people say this is the new frontier of digital property that will irrevocably change things forever. Skeptics say it's just a fad and that this bubble will burst very soon.

They are both right.

The majority of the new NFTs sold in this new explosion will eventually lose nearly all their value on the secondary market. A lot of what is happening is enthusiasm and FOMO, the fear of missing out. Most of these things being produced and sold right now will not be worth the electricity needed to process the transfer of ownership. However, many of them will remain extremely valuable.

Whether the massive number of trades happening right now will be profitable for particular individuals in 10 years is the least interesting thing about NFTs. This is much bigger than that. This technology that is rocketing into public awareness will be remembered as one of the most significant technological changes to intellectual property and media in our lifetimes. Most news outlets and books that are coming out right now aren't talking about why that is. Instead, they are focusing on the big numbers and get-rich-quick promises. Make no mistake: NFTs are a thing. They are sticking with us whether or not the owner of Beeple's art will make a profit off of that sale.

This book will tell you what NFTs are, why they are going to be a feature of regular people's lives, and how you can prepare yourself for this new reality and capitalize on it.

Chapter 1: What Is an NFT?

In the year 2015, the legendary rap group The Wu-Tang Clan generated a singularly unique idea. They produced an album for which there was only one copy in existence. They put it inside of a beautifully crafted box. They sold it at an auction to the highest bidder. That album was purchased by the so-called "pharma bro," Martin Shkreli for $2 million. Purchasing this album came with conditions. The owner was not allowed to make any copies of it or distribute it at all until 88 years after its release. The new owner would be allowed to have guests listen to it if they wanted to do that in their own home, but only in their home. It is an ultra-rare non-fungible physical asset. RZA, the informal leader of the Wu-Tang clan, produced what is perhaps the first real-life non-fungible token of music.

This is a very simple, clear example of what NFTs are. The only difference between Wu-Tang's one-of-a-kind album, *Once Upon a Time in Shaolin*, and a music NFT is that NFTs exist digitally, distributed over countless computer systems.

The Short Answer

The first and best question you probably have is, what is a non-fungible token? Or, specifically, what does *fungible* even mean? Fungibility is the quality of a thing's interchangeability and ease of replacement. A fungible thing is easily replaced with a copy. A non-fungible thing is not.

Take an example like a mass-produced T-shirt. T-shirts are created off of an assembly line, and most of them are exactly the same. If your T-shirt rips, you can order another one and it will be completely indistinguishable from the one you owned before. Something that is not fungible would be something like an original piece of art by Magritte. An original item, something that is one of a kind, is as non-fungible as it gets.

Now consider the following: that t-shirt that was replaced might not really be fungible. If that t-shirt had a great deal of sentimental value to that person, it would be fungible for everybody else, but very non-fungible for the owner. What if it was an ordinary white undershirt that you can buy in packs of 10 for a few dollars, but you got that shirt at a Red Hot Chili Peppers concert when the lead singer, Anthony Kiedis, took it off his body and threw it into the crowd, and you were the person who caught it. That makes it suddenly worth more than an ordinary shirt of the same design and manufacture. Now it has an experience attached to it, it has a celebrity attached to it. That shirt is more than just cotton fiber. That fungible shirt is now non-fungible.

The penultimate form of fungibility is cash. Any $20 bill can be replaced with any other $20 bill, or replaced with two $10s or four $5s. The primary reason money was invented is because of this fungibility. Money is an exchange medium, a way of quantifying value and allowing people to exchange goods and services easily. Before cash, gold was the standard medium of exchange; something valuable that is easy to trade, difficult to forge, and nonperishable.

Cryptocurrencies are also exchange mediums, like cash, but cryptos like Bitcoin and Ethereum are even more fungible than gold or cash. Any bitcoin is as good as any other bitcoin. They are perfectly fungible. Cash is only slightly less fungible, because they have different serial numbers on them, and theoretically you could be innocently holding a $20 bill that was stolen from a bank without knowing it. Trying to spend that bill with that serial number could lead to an uncomfortable conversation with the police through no fault of your own.

We learned back in the days of Napster that data is infinitely replicable. When music was on discs, you had to pay money to print discs. You had to print the cover art, produce the plastic cases, and use trucks and boats to move all the component parts and the final product between locations all over the world. When the final product went to market, there was limited shelf space. On the internet, a song in digital form can be copied hypothetically an infinite number of times and passed around to an infinite number of people, and the only cost is the server space and the electricity bill. Data of any kind is extremely fungible. As long as you can control the data from being corrupted, any copy of a song is replicable by an identical file, easily and cheaply.

In the traditional, real-world economy before the internet, the great challenge of humans was fighting scarcity. There are always limits on resources, talent, and time. There is only so much oil that can be produced. There are natural limits based on technology, skilled labor, geology, and the physical quantity that exists on the planet. There isn't an unlimited amount of oil and there isn't an unlimited amount that can be drilled on any given day. The internet doesn't work that way. Scarcity doesn't exist in a space of pure data.

Until now.

What cryptos do in general, and NFTs in particular, is add scarcity to a digital world without scarcity. NFTs offer a new frontier of digital scarcity, where one-of-a-kind digital assets exist and can be traded. That is the reason they have become a big deal and why reading this book is a good use of your time.

Fungibility and Value

To understand why NFTs and cryptocurrencies like Bitcoin and Ethereum are valuable, we have to talk about something a little abstract. We have to understand exactly what value is and where it comes from.

To be short about it, value comes from us. Value comes from what humans want. Value does not exist outside of us. Value doesn't exist intrinsically in things. Einstein's great observation was that an object's speed and direction in a space only makes sense in the context of other objects' speed and direction. In a completely black void, it would be impossible to determine the speed or the direction of the object's movement without other stuff like stars and planets to measure it against. Value and money work the same way. The value of a thing requires a comparison to other things. This sounds a bit heady right now, but this is much easier to understand than it seems at first.

What is a bottle of water worth? 16 oz of reverse-osmosis filtered water in a plastic bottle costs more in Nevada than it does in Michigan. There are a lot of factors involved in pricing, but in this case, the main issue is how much water is available. A bottle of water might cost $2 in Florida on an ordinary day. If Florida was slammed with a devastating hurricane that destroyed the roads and infrastructure, and overwhelmed the systems that deliver freshwater into homes, the price of clean water goes up considerably.

So what is an NFT worth? Intrinsically, nothing. Gold isn't worth anything intrinsically, either. A barrel of crude oil isn't worth anything, either. The value for these things comes from the fact that we value them for their use to us, and that's all. What was gold worth before smiths learned how to heat it and forge it into jewelry and art? Nothing. What was oil worth before the combustion engine was invented? Nothing. They became valuable the moment we found a use for them.

Some people will pay a considerable amount of money to buy gold jewelry to wear in public. Other people have no interest in gold, and wouldn't buy it or wear it. But if the person who doesn't like gold happens to have a lot of it, and knows someone who does want gold, they can sell that gold for whatever the buyer thinks is a fair price.

Follow that analogy through. There are a lot of reasons why NFTs should be of interest to you, but it ultimately doesn't matter if you see any value in them whatsoever. What matters is that other people find value in it, and they are willing to pay money for them, just like the buyer and seller of gold.

A New Age of Digital Property

Are you still confused about why someone would pay $69 million for a JPEG? This analogy should help you understand.

Consider a famous painting like *A Sunday Afternoon on the Island of La Grande Jatte* by Georges Seurat. That's the painting of all the fancy people dressed up nicely and hanging out in a park, but if you get up very close you can see that the image is just tiny dots. This very famous painting is in the possession of the Art Institute of Chicago and it is worth an estimated $650 million; considerably more than Beeple's piece.

You can find a JPEG of this famous French painting and download it for free. You could order a poster for around $20 and hang it on the wall. Yes, $20 for a copy. Not $650 million for a copy. A poster print isn't worth what the original is by a mile.

Allow us to ask a stupid question and then answer it: Why is the original painting worth so much but a copy is worthless? Because *it is the original*.

Consider a hypothetical, science fiction scenario. Imagine if there was a machine that could scan a painting and determine every exact brush stroke, then paint an exact replica, a perfect forgery down to the molecular level. The copy is so precise that the scanning machine couldn't tell them apart. Let's say this machine could produce thousands of these molecularly identical paintings in an assembly line.

Logically, the paintings would all have the same value. They are exactly the same. The only difference is that one is the original. That makes all the difference. The original painting would still be worth $650 million. The copies would be worth whatever slightly more expensive printed posters are worth.

Where things come from matters. The T-shirt worn by Anthony Keitis is valuable for no other reason than he wore it. An NFT is valuable because of who made it or owned it.

Chapter 2: Crypto & Ethereum

Not so long ago, it was common wisdom that internet dating was for losers. Now it is incredibly common and socially acceptable. The common wisdom is often wrong, and people who are quick to dismiss new movements are people who miss out on them. Ten years ago, Bitcoin was a brave and fun little experiment in technical libertarianism. Now major banks, corporations, governments, and hedge funds are taking cryptocurrency very, very seriously.

We have been promised a bubble burst in the crypto market, a doomsday scenario where everyone loses all of their money. It's been years, and there is no sign this will happen. Finance experts are now using cryptocurrencies to hedge against inflation and currency value fluctuations. The price of crypto goes up and down, sometimes quickly and dramatically, but over the long term, it always trends upwards.

To understand NFTs, first, we have to understand cryptocurrencies, particularly Ethereum (ETH).

What is Cryptocurrency?

If you talk to a computer guy about it, they might make crypto sound more complicated than it is. It's very simple, and anyone can understand it without jargon or technical terminology.

Cryptocurrency is not, technically, a currency. Courts have ruled on this and decided that it is a digital asset, not a currency. There are very important differences between the two, legally speaking, but we'll save that conversation for a later chapter. It is a store of value and a medium of exchange, just like gold used to be.

In the modern economy, most money exists *on* paper, not *as* paper. More money exists on computers owned by banks than exists as physical, paper cash. The entire reason why the economy can operate at the speed and efficiency it does is that banks are very good at recording this money and keeping vast ledgers of transactions. Whenever you buy something with a debit card, your bank communicates with the bank of whoever you are buying from. Your bank digitally subtracts the money from your account, and their bank digitally adds money to their customer's account. If these records didn't match, it would be a huge problem.

If you bought a burger for $5 and your bank subtracted $5 from your account, but the burger joint's bank added $100 to their account, suddenly a bank has added $95 to the money supply with a push of a button. Banks stay in business because they are very good at keeping these records straight. Any bank that couldn't do this competently would be out of business and employees could be looking at prison time.

This cashless economy is not new. It's ancient. Most money, for most of human history, did not exist in cash. Most of it existed on ledgers, just like at banks. A ledger is a list of purchases and sales. The oldest known ledger is a few thousand years old and written on clay (Dockrill, 2016).

If Brad bought a few 2 x 4s from Steve, Steve would write down a note in a book that they agreed that Brad would pay $100 for them. Both would sign it to verify that Steve wasn't forging a sale. Brad could leave with the 2 x 4s and cash never changed hands. The signatures are proof in case there is a dispute about it later. It's exactly how bank cards work, but in the past, the ledgers existed as several different people's personal ledgers. As long as everyone's balance sheet is in the black, no one goes looking for anyone to pay up what's owed. This system can work without cash for a long time, so long as the people trading this way can trust each other enough that they won't try to skip town and never settle up.

Modern banking works this same way but faster, digitally, and with much less need for trust between parties. What crypto does is keep a perfect ledger of transactions without the need for two banks or a payment processor. Crypto allows us to bypass three middlemen in the transaction. This is a phenomenally significant technology.

Cryptocurrencies like Ethereum and Bitcoin work by creating a very long, decentralized ledger known as a *blockchain*. Anytime a transaction takes place, a new entry is added to the ledger. Every few seconds, a new "block" of transactions is added. Each block refers to the previous block, thus stringing them together into a "chain." That's all the blockchain is. A series of ledger entries, just like a ledger book that we might have seen a few hundred years ago.

Like those old ledger books, the blockchain doesn't exist on any one computer. It exists on many computers. People who lend their computer power to maintain the blockchain functions are called "miners." Mining generates new crypto to miners as a reward for using electricity and computers for this task.

Any block that is created can never be changed. It is write-only. It is forever. Each time a block is added to the chain, mining computers all communicate with each other and have to reach a consensus. The computers compare their own blockchain records against others and check each other's work. If a new block in a chain doesn't match any other computer, the block is rejected. All the computers, working independently, work to keep each other honest.

The only way to hack and alter the chain would be to trick every computer checking the work at the same time, to hack every block in the chain after the earliest hacked block, and it would have to do it so fast that it could pull off this impossible feat before a single new block was added. This is only possible in science fiction. At this time, no one has even remotely the computing power necessary to hack the blockchain.

That was a lot of info to throw at you all at once, so we're going to bullet point the important parts to make sure it sinks in because you have to have a good grasp of this before we move on.

- Crypto is not money. It is an asset, like precious metals.

- Crypto exists on a blockchain, which is a very fancy and technical ledger. It's just a list of transactions of who gave who what and when.

- Crypto exists on many computers all over the world that collaborate to keep the system working and free of counterfeiting.

Why Crypto is Valuable

A better question is, "Why is cash valuable?" After all, cash is just paper. Cash's value comes from its use as a medium of exchange, the fact that anyone will accept cash from a solvent mint, and most importantly: to do business in a country, you have to pay to do business there with their money. Governments only accept their own currency for taxes.

Crypto is valuable for similar reasons, but it doesn't have the full faith and credit of any government. We discussed earlier where value comes from. Certain things with certain qualities at certain times will necessarily be valuable. Crypto has certain intrinsic qualities that give them advantages over other kinds of traditional state-printed fiat currency or gold.

For one thing, crypto is completely out in the open. There is no hiding in a blockchain world. The data on the blockchain is publicly available. Anyone can look at it. With everything running down in calculations on ledgers, no one is hiding the ball, no one can embezzle, no one can move money without it being noticed.

Because the ownership of crypto-wallets is anonymous, this lends itself well for privacy-concerned people who don't want to be under the eye of governments or corporations that like to track the ways we spend our money. This could be for completely valid, legal reasons. It can also be used for dark money financing and illegal activities like sales of drugs or weapons. Any kind of market transaction, black, white, or grey, can be anonymous so long as the wallet-owner's ID is safely guarded. You don't need a credit check or a photo ID to buy and sell crypto. The normal restrictions that banks have to alert the government when they see red flags don't exist here.

Those who are suspicious and skeptical of government power and monetary policy often bring up the fact that crypto is predictably inflationary. When using any kind of state-backed currency, a nation's monetary policy is operated by people who are experts, but fallible. They can do their best, but as we have seen in history, when they fail it can be quite disastrous. A government can increase or decrease the money supply by tweaking its central bank's interest rates. When the government increases the supply of money, there is usually a corresponding inflation of prices, as more cash is chasing fewer goods. This is not a problem for a respectable and solvent cryptocurrency. A cryptocurrency like Ethereum has a very predictable inflationary schedule.

"What about NFTs?" you might be asking. "What does Bitcoin or Ethereum have to do with NFTs?"

I'm glad you asked, because we are just coming to that.

Digital assets like Bitcoin and Ethereum exist in their own blockchains. They are separate things. Most NFTs exist on Ethereum's blockchain, or an "alt-coin" chain that is built using Ethereum. One thing that makes Ethereum special is that it can store any digital data on its blockchain. That includes videos, music, images, documents, or anything else that can be stored on a computer. Bitcoin can't do that.

Those digital items, like images and music, are the NFTs. The blockchain is what makes NFTs what they are and what makes them special.

Ethereum and Smart Contracts

Bitcoin is presently the #1 cryptocurrency, with Ethereum close behind it at #2.

One thing that makes Ethereum very special is that it offers something called smart contracts. A smart contract is just like a legal contract, but it is written in computer code and it is handled by computers, without any need for lawyers or judges. A smart contract is an automatically executing contract. Any crypto asset can have a smart contract attached to it. The implications of this technology are massive, but we'll wait to dive deeper into that later on. The important part to understand right now is that property rights and contracts can be added indelibly to the digital property itself. This is crucial to why NFTs are more than just expensive art digitally assigned to a digital address and why Ethereum is crucial in this story.

Ethereum is a much more developed technology than Bitcoin. Ethereum powers and maintains virtual spaces like The Sandbox and DeFi space. The Sandbox is a brave experiment in building a virtual world entirely on a blockchain, in which users who add and develop the space are rewarded with their own internal crypto called SAND. These rewards also come from making and contributing NFTs. DeFi is short for "decentralized finance," which refers to any of this new blockchain finance technology and the platforms that run on them.

Ethereum is also used to run blockchain domains and NFT marketplaces. Of the top 100 most-used cryptocurrencies, more than half are built on Ethereum's ERC-20 token standard. Most of these "alt-coin" chains also use Ethereum's ERC-721 standard for NFTs. "Standard" here means the interoperability of the underlying code. That's a lot of confusing words that can be explained with an analogy. There is a standard electrical outlet in America, the three-holed wall socket. You use it for most things in your home. Every electrical object you can buy will fit that wall socket. No matter what it is. It can be a lamp, a television, a computer, or a toaster. They all work perfectly with that standard outlet. When everyone has the same outlet standard, everyone can build products for it easily because they are *interoperable*. Each company doesn't have a different type of plug for a different type of outlet. However, those same products won't work in many places in Europe. The US and Europe use different standards that are not interoperable. A token standard is the same idea. All the different crypto assets work on the same blockchain so long as they follow the same standard. ERC-20 is the fungible standard. ERC-721 is the non-fungible standard.

Ethereum's interoperability between assets means that things can be built by interconnecting them in very interesting ways. That brings us to smart contracts, which is what it's all about. Anything a computer can do, a contract can do. The new, hot smart contract is a built-in way of paying out royalties. Intrinsic to the NFT is code that executes automatically every time the token is sold; an NFT with this contract pays out a percentage to the original creator. This means deposits into the artist's crypto wallet from now until forever. The most famous case of this was done by an early NFT adopter, Imogen Heap.

Smart contracts are part of the NFT. They cannot be changed or removed. These royalty payments are just the start of what is possible. This removes the ability or need to take disputes to courts of law. The computer executes the code and it happens. There are no notaries, there are no expensive lawyers to argue their cases in front of judges, there is no case law and legal interpretation of the code. There are no renegotiations with record labels or messy, public disputes. The contracts just happen.

Sports athletes often have tragic lives after retirement. Many blow their money while they are young and don't prepare for the future. They don't save money, they don't use their money wisely, as young people often do. NFTs could be a lifeline for people like this. Residuals trickling in from their career days could help them after retirement, through smart contracts.

Ethereum has limitations, but developers are in the process of solving them. At this time, Ethereum is the only real game in town when it comes to NFTs.

Chapter 3: The Market

Those who are jumping into the NFT market right now are doing so in an exciting time, with a lot of promise and a little bit of chaos. This is very new and the market and technology are changing rapidly. No one can say with certainty what things will look like in a few years, which adds to the risk, but also the fun.

Understanding how the market operates, how to capitalize on opportunities, and how to prepare for the future are all going to be important. This book teaches you the bare basics but for people who want to get involved, you will need to do your own research and continue to learn in a marketplace that is always evolving.

Who Wants In?

There are as many reasons to get into the crypto and NFT market as there are people, and you don't need a lot of money to get started. NFTs offer opportunities for investors, speculators, collectors, content creators, publicists, advertisers, and every business adjacent to the primary market. In short, anyone who has taken the time to understand this market sees the potential and wants in.

One feature of NFTs that is very undersold is that they are just fun. There are tons of them and the internet has become an enormous garage sale of strange and unique things that you can buy, sell, and swap. It's fun for the same reason a garage sale is. You never can tell what you'll find when you walk up to someone's driveway and start looking through their junk. Sometimes you'll find something great. Sometimes you'll find something that has no market value, but you just love it anyway and you're happy to pay a few dollars for it. For a lot of people, buying and selling art is just more fun than buying and selling stocks.

There is a grand tradition in music fandom to declare that you liked a band before they got big. You saw a group like The Doors when they were still playing in bars in southern California before they had a record contract. What if you could prove that you liked them before they were big? What if you could prove that you saw the potential in a professional fighter like Jon Jones before he won his first belt by owning one of his NFTs dated to show when you got it? If bragging rights are something that you value, that's something to consider.

Content Creators

The new digital era of music has given new artists opportunities to bypass the traditional cultural gatekeepers and go directly to potential fans. That's very exciting in large part, because the money in music and art is not what it used to be.

Musician Jacques Greene's hit single, "Another Girl," has netted 7 million listens on Spotify. That earned him $27,904 in royalties from the platform spread out over 10 years. For contrast, he sold a single animated GIF for 13 ETH, which was worth a little over $16,037.32 at the time. He made five years' worth of royalties in a matter of minutes. (Beck, 2021)

You can see why there is a tremendous amount of excitement from many content creators of all different types of genres and skills. NFTs offer them a way to sell exclusive collectibles and merchandise directly to the public and bypass intermediaries. Musicians previously had to rely on recording studios and record labels; they have now become reliant on Silicon Valley music-streaming services. Likewise, filmmakers who were previously dependent on the fickle Hollywood studio system, are now dependent on services like Netflix and YouTube. Visual artists were reliant on galleries and now work through platforms like DeviantArt.

Artists were able to free themselves from one monolith only to be dragged into a new one. The new system offers them certain advantages, but there are also a lot of problems with these new digital controllers.

NFTs are the newest opportunity to completely bypass the powers-that-be.

Investment

There are a lot of reasons that a person might want to collect a piece of art. One is that they tend to retain their value and grow it over time. It is a very safe way to store value and hedge against inflation. The older the piece is, and the more famous the artist, the more valuable they tend to be. This is one reason why rich people fill their houses with expensive art. Not just because they enjoy it, but also because it is a safe piece in their portfolio.

Another reason is simply bragging rights. You could display art at your home for guests to let them know that you are a cultured person who has good taste. It means you have the resources to decorate your home with things like famous art and are willing to take on the tremendous responsibility of caretaking for a valuable piece of art. A lot of art that is privately owned is also loaned out to museums to show publicly, and somewhere in the little placard next to the piece of art it will show who owns it and that they are lending it out. This gives a sense that they are not selfish with their item; they are willing to share it with the world.

There may be some kind of bragging rights for having a 4% share in the next Kanye West song. And in the same way that you might hang a painting on your wall, you could open your phone and show your proof of ownership for that song to a person. In social environments, we are constantly transmitting and receiving signals that operate on a subconscious level. How we dress and what kind of vehicle we drive sends information to others, deliberately or not. Even our posture or ability to maintain eye contact communicates things about us to others. Owning a share of a valuable NFT can do the same. It can be a way of signaling something you want others to see about you. Many women pay top dollar to have the word "Gucci" on their purses. People will do the same for an NFT if they believe it will tell others something about who they are.

NFTs are already being used as collateral for loans. You can put up an NFT to borrow cryptocurrency. You can turn that crypto into cash. You could short it, loan it, wait for a market tumble, and buy it back on the cheap to get your NFT back. You could leverage it in any number of ways. NFTs have become a legitimate, although often volatile, financial tool.

Don't be surprised to see our 401ks diversify into bluechip NFTs. Soon, all of us will likely be slightly invested in NFTs.

Investing in NFTs isn't just about buying NFTs. Stock values for companies that have been successful selling NFTs have seen spikes in shareholder value. When a company shows successful involvement in a blockchain asset, pay attention. Stock prices for Dolphin Entertainment and Hall of Fame Resort & Entertainment doubled after they began investing in the NFT market (C, 2021).

Speculation

Making money speculating requires special knowledge or a hunch about the future that others don't share. Speculation can be as random as gambling, but people with deep insight into trends and a strong sense of things to come can use this skill with NFTs the same as they do with any other investment. If you can predict what people will care about a few years in the future, NFTs need to be on your radar.

An NFT's value is usually based on the identity of the signature on it. There's an opportunity for speculators who are quick to identify a rising star and take the chance to produce, purchase, and hold an NFT based on their expected future output. For example, a very promising high school athlete might produce an NFT. At a later date, a person might purchase that NFT. Now assume that young person's career is very successful; they have an impressive career in college, and then go on to professional sports. If a person purchased this kind of NFT from a superstar at a very low cost before they were big, they would have something that could become enormously valuable.

This is one of the many strange and moral conundrums that NFTs require us to think about. Consider what it means if a talent scout for a university were able to persuade a high school athlete to sell them an NFT for $500. Is this a form of insider trading? Probably not. A scout could get a signature from a high schooler on a football and wouldn't have any legal worries in the future. People who are close to an industry and have an insider's understanding can use that knowledge. Since there haven't been any court rulings on this yet, we can't know for certain what the law says about this. If it is perfectly legal, there might be new regulations and laws to address this. That's a risk in speculation. There are a lot of risks and a lot of rewards.

Chapter 4: Causes for Concern

It's not all wine and roses. There are reasons to be hesitant, even if you are well-informed and see the potential. Everything has downsides, and NFTs and cryptocurrencies are no exception to this rule. There is a lot of alarmism and exaggeration about the dangers of crypto markets. Most are overblown, but even the ones that are overstated have their merits. It's necessary to address these because problems aren't solved until they are acknowledged.

Energy and Pollution

Recently there has been a lot of new attention paid to the amount of energy used to maintain blockchains. Blockchain is a very clever and valuable technology, but it is energy inefficient. Whereas two banks can send a tiny bit of data to one another, the blockchain requires a lot of very powerful computers using a tremendous amount of power to compete with each other.

If you've read news headlines recently, this issue probably seems noncontroversial. News makes money by eliciting clicks with enticing headlines, and nuanced discussions don't generate the same amount of traffic as doom and gloom stories. That said, the facts of the issue of pollution are not a consensus. There is a vigorous debate on this topic, with both sides of the issue making strong points that need to be considered.

Most of this news comes from one source, an academic article in the journal *Nature Climate Change*. This 2018 article raised alarms that Bitcoin alone could raise the global temperature by 2 degrees Celsius within the next 30 to 60 years, enough to begin raising the ocean to catastrophic levels (Dittmar & Praktiknjo, 2019).

Because the authors are experts on climate science and not computer science, they make some assumptions that aren't reliable. For one, the authors assume that exponential adoption of crypto will continue indefinitely. That is far from a certainty. Few things grow exponentially forever, unabated. Almost all growth has peaks and valleys, and periods of flattening.

The article also makes a major mistake in saying that the Bitcoin network processes 1 billion processes, which is several times more than what Bitcoin can do. It also assumes that each transaction equals one block. As we discussed earlier, a single block contains many transactions; as many as 3,000 per block for Bitcoin.

The article claims that a single Bitcoin transaction requires more electricity than 750,000 credit card swipes. This is true, but electronic banking transactions are a lot more than just signals sent by swipes at retailers. Banks and credit card companies have an infrastructure. They have offices, they have company cars, ATMs, customer service systems, and many other things that also use energy but aren't factored into the calculations.

The numbers also assume that Bitcoin energy comes exclusively from fossil fuels. Many crypto mining operations use coal as their primary energy source for a considerable amount of the work they do. This is without a doubt something that is troubling and needs to be phased out, but it isn't particular to computing. The point is that the numbers require that ALL energy is spent this way, which isn't true.

Miners are incentivized to reduce the cost of mining by reducing energy. At a certain point, if energy expenses are too high, mining profits are at a net loss, and mining would end. The energy efficiency of mining equipment has been improving, though the paper doesn't address this.

The exact figures of how much energy is consumed aren't known for sure, and estimates range between 40-440Terawatts-hour per year. According to Cambridge, their best guess is about 130TWh (CBECI, 2021), which is the same as the energy spent mining gold every year.

There are also some very interesting ideas about how to make crypto more green. Computer farms of the sort that miners use produce a considerable amount of heat from the electricity they consume and these miners are already developing ways to use that heart as a form of energy itself.

Renewable energy has a lot of promise, but at this time they have a technological chokepoint that stops them from becoming the standard. Solar and wind energy can pull tremendous amounts of energy if the sun is shining and the wind is blowing, much more than is needed on the electrical grid all at once. When the sun isn't shining and the wind isn't blowing, it produces nothing. At this time, we don't have the technology to store vast amounts of energy. That amount of battery storage necessary isn't feasible yet. During those peak times, that excess energy could be directed specifically to mining, and the crypto produced could be invested back into the energy company towards expanding renewables.

Don't take this to mean that crypto has no impact on the environment. That isn't true at all. There are legitimate concerns about this issue, but it is not likely the climate doomsday scenario that news headlines imply it is.

Bubbles

Crypto is not regulated like banks are. We are at the later stages of a Wild West crypto economy. The market has a lot of natural volatility and the potential to be manipulated by governments and private citizens with the money to throw their weight around.

Tweets sent by people like Elon Musk can spike or tank the crypto market by enormous margins (Kau, 2021). This can be accidental or deliberate. One way to manipulate the market for profit is for a "whale," a well-financed person or institution, to purchase a lot of crypto. They need a lot of money to make this happen, but if coins are being bought up quickly and in large quantities, the price will spike. It creates a shortage and reinforces people's confidence in the value of the asset, and more people want to get in on the action, also increasing the value. The whale's portfolio will go up. When they see it leveling off, the whale can dump their portfolio for a lot of money, which tanks the price. People see it going down and panic sell. Now that the price is low again, the whale can buy it up cheap. They can repeat this process forever. It would be naive to assume governments aren't participating.

Bubbles are an unavoidable feature of any market, but crypto especially. This is a very new thing, and it is unregulated and still in its infancy. The traditional legacy banking system has put enormous resources into learning how to calculate risk, how to hedge it, how to maximize profits, and develop an enormous library of financial instruments to maximize profit and keep the market stable enough that they feel secure to operate in it with minimal risk. Crypto is not quite so mature. It is more like a young person kicking in the door and claiming that the old people don't know what they are talking about and trying to change everything all at once. The crypto culture is right about a lot of things and they're also probably wrong about a lot of things. A certain amount of time needs to go by, and an amount of learning is necessary before this thing works itself out.

Legal Grey Area

During times of great economic crisis, people are often eager to find alternatives to the economic system that is in crisis. During the great depression and stock market crash in America in the 1930s, there was a fear that government policies and spending would lead to hyperinflation of the kind experienced in Germany. To protect themselves from poor government monetary policy, people with the means to do so attempted to turn their cash into commodities, particularly gold. Even if the value of cash is devalued, the relative price of other assets like land and gold rise by the same amount, protecting the person from having their entire savings withered away by central banks.

The value of any currency is dependent on people's trust and faith in it. If people begin to jettison cash, the value of that country's cash diminishes. Cash is similar to any other asset. It has a supply and demand curve just like anything else. When people lose faith in the solvency and profitability of a corporation, the stock value plummets. When people lose faith in the solvency and future of a country, the value of its money vanishes.

The United States government was not naive to this fact. For that reason, they wanted to get ahead of the curve and decided that they had the right and responsibility to confiscate gold. In their mind, if no one had a means of exiting the United States dollar, the value of it couldn't be destabilized quite so easily. They also instituted many financial regulations, some sensible, some crazy, to protect the United States dollar.

Make no mistake. If the United States dollar seems threatened by cryptocurrency, governments will intervene and shut it down. This includes NFTs. A problem with regulating digital assets is that the regulators don't know anything about computers. The average age for a senator in the United States is 64 years old (Cillizza, 2021). Almost all of them have backgrounds in the military or law. There are little to no politicians with a strong background in technology, except perhaps the 2020 presidential candidate, Andrew Yang, who is not an elected official at the time of this writing.

Other countries, without warning or a deep understanding of what is happening, have begun to crack down on digital assets. In a recent case, India has outlawed cryptocurrencies entirely. This is a response to a technology that they fear the consequences and implications of, and they view outlawing these currencies as getting a head start on it before it gets out of their control. China has simultaneously begun to develop its own cryptocurrency, outlaw competing currencies, and begin to invest in current cryptocurrencies that are already popular and proven and in circulation at this time. This is a sign that China has a good sense of the implications of what crypto is and wants to get a lockdown on it and control it.

There's no reason to think that United States governments or any governments in the West will not also begin investigating and regulating these things. On account of the general ignorance of these issues by the governments and by the voters, we can expect that whenever regulation does come our way will be guided by established institutions with deep pockets who have a reason to be concerned about a fledgling upstart that plans on putting them out of business through obsolescence. This is something that everyone needs to seriously consider before going deeply into investment in NFTs or crypto. There's a lot of instability in these markets intrinsically because it is a new technology that people are still figuring out and constantly reinventing, but there's an additional layer of instability in the unpredictable reactions from the government. Government tends to operate at two speeds: "Do nothing" and "overreact." If senators aren't placed into a state of panic in a hurry, they usually don't do anything. When they do act, you can expect an overreaction.

Copyright and Illegal Content

Making an NFT doesn't automatically give you a copyright to the art. Likewise, tokenizing Disney's *Snow White and the Seven Dwarves* into a video NFT doesn't mean you have the right to it, either. There isn't much to stop people from tokenizing material that they have no right to and spreading it.

NFT trading websites use software to check for copyrighted material and to pull it down in case it is reported. That's all well and good, except for one very important thing. The blockchain is forever. If someone uploads something onto it, the chain can't be altered. That material can't be wiped. Enforcement of copyright is very difficult.

It isn't clear yet how courts will rule on the copyrights of copying NFTs, and if purchasing an NFT implies ownership of intellectual property. There is currently a lot of speculation that patent trolls are buying NFTs believing they can win that fight in court. A "patent troll" is a pejorative for a person who makes a living by suing companies with often frivolous claims of patent ownership. IBM is currently trying to tokenize patents, although what that means exactly isn't clear (Mollen, 2021).

Assets VS Currency

As we discussed earlier, crypto is not considered a form of currency, legally speaking, even though it can be traded as fluidly as digital cash.

Because cryptos of any kind, including NFTs, are assets, that makes them subject to capital gains taxes. A capital gains tax requires a declaration of assets that have increased in value and a tax based on that increase, even before any taxes on a sale of the NFT. Putting real money into NFTs means you need to keep your documentation solid to avoid any potential attention from tax collection agencies, particularly if you strike it big.

Lots of products have taxes specific to them, and a lot of political and economic considerations are used in crafting these policies. There's no reason that the tax rate can't be adjusted specifically to target this market.

Covenant Contracts

This is a legal issue that hasn't been publicly discussed yet, but is likely to arrive sooner rather than later. About a hundred years ago and earlier there was a concept in contract law called *exclusionary covenants*. These were ruled unconstitutional by the United States Supreme Court. The way that these covenants worked is that when a contract was signed to sell a house, they would include a clause that the new owner would not be allowed to sell the house to a black person, and they were required to also include that same clause when they sold it in the future.

In effect, this deal made a particular house and a piece of land permanently and irrevocably barred from the possession of any black person forever. A contract between two people could lock up a piece of land until the end of time. For obvious reasons, this was considered unconstitutional. Besides being racist, why should any person have a right to control a product or piece of land for thousands of years after they are dead?

The smart contracts forwarded by Ethereum blockchain may be running into a very similar problem in the courts. Because the smart contracts are locked into perpetuity, theoretically if Ethereum lasted a thousand years, then the rules made now will force people to live by them long after any of the original parties are still alive.

These kinds of issues are difficult for lawyers and computer scientists to wrap their heads around. Trying to explain this in front of a court to people who don't know the first thing about computers is a challenge that will only get worse as our lives become more entangled with machines that are too complicated for the ordinary person to understand. Judges are experts in law. They don't know the first thing about computers.

Scams

Not all cryptos and services are made equal.

There are few cryptocurrencies and blockchains that are tried and true and respected and have earned the trust of investors. You've heard of a few of them. You may not know that there are countless others.

Making a new crypto currency is as easy as copying the work others have already done, and people do it all the time. Even pro-boxer Manny Pacquiao made his own cryptocurrency. Digital currencies are being developed faster than can be tracked. Some of these are small, unheard of, but legitimate. Some are complete and utter scams that promise to make you Bitcoin-rich in a short amount of time, and in fact, will just take your money and run.

To know the difference, you have to keep an eye out for what is and is not respected. If you are interested, you can always go and find the white paper and read it for yourself. When a person or a company launches a new cryptocurrency, they almost always release a whitepaper. These documents outline the information about what the crypto is and what it's goals are. This includes technical information about how it works, usually including problems with other crypto assets that this new asset is attempting to solve. They contain financial and commercial information to help attract investors. These documents are usually in plain language so you don't need to be an expert to understand them.

Most cryptocurrency such as Ethereum or Bitcoin generate more coins automatically, but some are created entirely at the whim of the creator of the coin. They can simply will the crypto into existence with the push of a button and wait for the price to reach whatever amount that they want, and then sell off their assets, dump the market, and move on to another project before doing it again. This game has happened several times. Everyone who did not get Bitcoin in its first few years regrets it now, and nobody wants to be the person to miss out on the next Bitcoin. Nobody wants to be the person that didn't buy a half dozen Bitcoin for pennies to become a multimillionaire 7 years later.

There have been a few custodial services that have taken the money and run after promising unrealistic return investments. Confidence games typically rely on the con artist making promises that are so big that the mark gets greedy and ignores the risks. Consider the Turkish CEO Faruk Faith Ozer. His company, Thodex, ran a major attention-grabbing promotion by selling Dogecoin at 75% under market value during Dogecoin's meteoric rise. It should surprise nobody that Thodex didn't have the Dogecoin, but they took people's money all the same. At the time of this writing, the Turkish Central bank has outlawed the use of cryptocurrency for payments of any goods or services as a response.

Gas Fees

Gas is the general reference for approximate transaction fees on the Ethereum blockchain. Gas is the cost of doing business with ETH. It is a fee, paid in ETH, to miners for their labor of computing transactions on the network.

The gas price is found in a sort-of auction system. Miners can pick which transactions to run, and give priority to those who are offering the highest amount for the transaction. The backlog is processed in descending order. Imagine going to a restaurant and ordering your meal, but you choose your price. Whoever offers to pay the most for dinner is served first. As diners leave and enter, those who low-balled their offer might find themselves waiting a very, very long time to eat.

Gas prices change all the time. The more activity there is in the market, the higher the prices can be expected, as traders have to auction to get priority in a very busy room.

The system works this way to incentivize miners to compete by adding more computer power to the network. The more computer power operating on the network, the faster transactions can move, and the more security the blockchain has, since the only way to break the security would be to have an even larger amount of computer power coordinated to actively undermine the entire system, which is unrealistic.

Gas prices have always been a feature of Ethereum that turns people off. This system puts a limit on its ability to quickly scale to meet demand.

Ethereum's developers have promised that the gas problem should be resolved using Ethereum 2.0's new (and hopefully improved) staking system for the same reason that it should reduce environmental impact: less computing power means less energy means less pollution.

Chapter 5: Art and Music

We are seeing a new and strange art renaissance, the same way we saw pointillism, expressionism, pop art, or dada. NFTs have generated a new crypto art movement, Trash Art. A whole new subculture has developed around crypto art and interesting computer-based art experiments.

A lot of artists are very excited for the potential of NFTs for income, but also for innovation through smart contracts.

Digital Rights of Artists

We learned back in the days of Napster that data is infinitely replicable. When music was on discs, you had to pay money to print discs, to print art for them, to put them into plastic cases, to put them on shelf space, and trucks to move them. On the internet, a song could be copied hypothetically an infinite number of times and passed around to an infinite number of people, and the only cost is the server space and the electricity bill.

Apple managed to solve this problem by offering songs at the cost of $1 each. At the time, music pirating was considered a serious threat by the music industry. However, the solution may have been worse than the initial problem. For the artists, moving the music into a $1 per song format crystallized in consumer's minds that a song is worth $1. People no longer had to purchase an entire album for $20. They could pick and choose one or two songs from an album that they liked, usually the ones that were big hits, and ignore the rest. This is great for consumers who didn't want to have to commit to an entire album, but it cut deeply into the pockets of recording artists.

But things got even worse after that. As the internet's infrastructure grew and was able to feed more and more data extremely quickly through widespread adoption of broadband internet, streaming services have become the standard. Netflix began as a delivery rental service that physically sent DVDs to your house. Netflix was ahead of the curve and anticipated that streaming was the future, and invested heavily into it. Now their name is synonymous with video streaming. You can see it in the very term "Netflix and chill." It's not "Amazon Prime and chill," it's not "Hulu and chill." While streaming services were taking over the video market, they also took over music, with wireless services through cell phones able to pipe streaming into every person's pocket at a relatively affordable rate.

The way recording artists are paid in this new world is in fractions of pennies off of individual listens. If a musician gets 100,000 listens through services such as YouTube music or Spotify, they get ridiculously low margins. At this point, it is effectively impossible to become a rock star of the sort that was legendary in the 1950s through the 1990s. An exceptionally rare few people ever make it big in music. Today, that rare few are even tinier.

One possible application of NFT's could bypass this new system that has made money for Silicon Valley, but taken a large toll on the musicians and artists themselves. Distribution has always been an extremely profitable business. People can create wonderful things, but if they cannot get them to people, they may as well not exist as far as the market is concerned.

We now have more and more means of bypassing the distribution choke points. Before, to get a contract, you would need to persuade some person with money that you could make them more money. This is no longer the case. Musicians such as Takeshi Six N9ne can make their videos themselves using just a cell phone, record their music using inexpensive equipment that's available for purchase online, and distribute their music themselves through a medium such as YouTube or Spotify. The gatekeepers have been removed. NFTs might offer a very important new way of bypassing the obstacle of middlemen whose job is to simply move the products to within arms reach of other people. With NFT's, artists can organize more contracts to control their music themselves and not be at a disadvantage during a negotiation. They don't need to negotiate anymore.

Safe Value

Most art created in most of human history isn't very good. That's a fact of life. Most artistic endeavors are failures, even the ones created by successful and talented people. There are countless TV shows that never got past the pilot phase of production. Many of the ones that got on the air had a season or less before being cancelled. Taking on production of a TV show is risky for the investors. Audiences are fickle, and there's no good way to predict what will be popular and what won't. It's not risky, however, for the actors and writers who gain experience, contacts, and items to add to their resumes.

NFTs work the same way. For the artist, producing an NFT costs only as much as the gas fee. That is all the investment they have to make into it. The risk and rewards for investors can be tremendous. NFTs are always a safe option for creators.

Even if they don't expect a sale, making an NFT might still be a good idea. If their day finally comes and their name gets some buzz, an original NFT of an early work that is a couple years old will suddenly look very interesting. For an artist, it could be a doodle on a napkin at a restaurant. It's not worth much now, but that could be worth something down the road if their career takes off.

IP and Smart Contracts

In the current digital age, intellectual property (IP) is more valuable than oil. The phenomenal success of the Marvel superhero movies goes to one company: whoever owns the IP. No one else can make a superhero movie with those characters. No one else can cash in on that franchise, and it is all about franchises.

This is why digital piracy was such a hot topic in the 2000s, and why patent theft by foreign competitors is a constant concern with no clear solution. The time, energy, and money it takes to develop a new technology, a new fiction franchise, a music career, are all immense. Not only are the stakes high, but stealing digital IP is incredibly easy.

Do you want to know what the secret recipe to make Coca-cola is? You can put a drop into a mass spectrometer and it will tell you everything in Coke and in what quantity. You now have the secret recipe. You might get in trouble if you tried selling that in America, but no one will stop you if you sell it in Russia. That recipe is what makes Coke valuable. If anyone can take it and copy it, how could they stay in business?

Art, music, movies, and television all have the same concerns. NFTs are a way for artists to sell something that can't be replicated. The product can be copied, but not the metadata. The value cannot be replicated, forged, stolen, or destroyed. Using smart contracts on NFTs looks like it might hold the solution to IP theft for people whose livelihoods depend on IP rights being respected.

Chapter 6: Sports and eSports

There is one place where nerd culture and jock culture overlap: collecting.

There was a very interesting and innovative video game that was available in Japanese arcades some decades ago called Sega Card Gen '10. The idea was that it was a baseball video game where you would insert baseball cards into the machine like you would a dollar bill into a vending machine, and those cards would then create your lineup. You bought the cards just like any other cards at any collectibles shop. Based on the baseball players' records, the video game estimated the players' performance in the game itself. So having more accomplished players with better stats would help you win in the video game. This genre still is popular in Asia, with perhaps the most successful current form as Sangokushi Taisen.

The potential of cards continues, but without the actual physical object being necessary. You could, for example, combine NFT trading cards with a very valuable video game property such as the MLB series, and those collectibles would allow you to have a stronger team in the video game. The game itself would incentivize the trading of players' cards. And for people who have no interest in video games it still increases the value, because as long as there are people who do play video games, they are willing to pay for these sorts of things.

NFT's Origins

NFTs were born strangely out of the video game universe. Video games have become incredibly large, expensive, and technically impressive endeavors. Video games have eclipsed Hollywood in terms of money as of a few years ago (Witkowski, 2020). The problem with video games is that they are incredibly risky businesses. You can spend hundreds of millions on it, and the thing can completely fail in an enormously large and competitive arena. These games take years of man-hours of people who are paid handsomely for their technical professional work.

One problem with video games traditionally, is that you sell them and then they are done. You spend all that time and resources to create something, then a number of people buy them, and then the project is over and you have to start on something new and take those same risks all over again.

Video game production studios have slowly introduced ways to make games long-term profitable. One of the pioneers of this way of doing business was a game that's still played today despite being years old. It's called Team Fortress 2. This game makes its money by selling players things that don't exist in the physical world. Effectively, they are selling NFTs for the game. In the game, you might be playing as a character who shoots a rocket launcher. However, if you pay the studio that produced the game the low, low price of two actual dollars, you could have a different kind of gun for your character in the game.

The studio that owns TF2, Valve, has the power to give every single person a copy of any gun or costume for any character that they want at any time. Because they have absolute control over the game and what's in it, they have the power to inject scarcity into it. This idea has evolved even more as items in these kinds of games are given very precise rarity. Some are extremely difficult to find, and some can only be acquired during very small windows, creating a natural limit on the quantity and circulation. These make-believe items can be traded and sold in a marketplace that is also owned by the company, where they get a taste of every transaction.

Some of these items might be cosmetic, they might have some kind of impact on the experience of the game, and some of them are just to change the aesthetic and make it look prettier. People pay very real money for this in vast amounts. This allows a game to stay profitable for years and years after the initial release, as they introduce new make-believe items into their marketplace and can keep on the same staff with the same experience on this project without shifting them onto something completely new.

So when you look at it like that, NFTs have already been around in some form or another, and are already making a lot of people a lot of money.

Rebirth of Sports Collectibles

This new form of digital assets has opened up a tremendous new enthusiasm for sports collectibles.

In the same way that people enjoy having a signed copy of something, this is a way of creating digital signatures. Payton Manning can take his collection of Super Bowl rings, make a 3D digitized model of them all by waving a 3D scanner near them, and then sell those 3D models.Someone may have already thought of this and started similar sales before this book was even published.

NBA Top Shot has made $230 million in sales in the last two years selling NFTs. A short video of LeBron James dunking on Nemanja Bjelica sold for $208,000. People are paying crazy sums of money for these things.

We are seeing the comeback of sports cards. They can be created with limited availability in the same way that art prints are. You might find an art print with a little notation that it is print number seven of 200. This indicates to anyone looking at it that only 200 of this particular print exist and that it is a rare thing to have. They can produce a limited number of Mickey Mantle digital cards, with maybe only a few hundred in existence. And this sort of asset could be easily traded with others the same way that kids and adults used to trade baseball cards not too long ago. And the internet market is quite a bit different because every single card is always in mint condition.

These assets can also be bundled with smart contracts in interesting ways. For example, a one-of-a-kind Wayne Gretzky card might also entitle the owner to a discount on all Wayne Gretzky merchandise sold on the NHLs online store. A card could entitle the owner to great seats at a game. Adding these features also increases the card's value far beyond just collectibility. NFTs could be integrated into fantasy sports leagues as a way of trading players by trading cards. It adds real function.

At this moment, the most important value that comes from an NFT is the non-fungibility, as we discussed earlier, but also the real person who created it. An unknown artist who develops an NFT and sells it can't expect it to be worth a lot. Jeff, the dental hygienist from Cincinnati Ohio, is not going to have a very profitable NFT just because his name is on it. An immensely successful and famous person, such as a politician or artist or athlete who makes an NFT, gives it tremendous value. As we said, NFTs are digital signatures and the signature is what matters.

This is going to be very profitable for many celebrities, particularly celebrities in a field that has developed a strong culture of memorabilia collection. That means especially sports and geek culture-related properties are smart to be doing what they are doing.

Video Game Assets

Video game assets have been commodified for years. This is particularly noticeable in the mobile games market. In these environments, players can often use fake in-game money which can be purchased as assets within the game. This in-game currency can be earned by playing the game, but it can also be earned by spending actual real money. And people do this all the time. Mobile games are cheap to make and easy for casual players to adopt, and they are extremely lucrative.

One kind of asset that is very popular in games is the "skin." A skin is essentially a different way of dressing up your avatar. An avatar is the character that you control in the game. If you are playing Super Mario Bros, Mario is your avatar. For many of these games, you are looking through the eyes of the Avatar; you're experiencing the game in the first person. This means that you don't even see your skin. Only other players see your skin while you're playing the game. You don't even enjoy the aesthetic that you earned or paid for.

Consider the implication of that for a moment. People will pay real money to change their appearance for others. They hardly get to enjoy it. Some of these skins are particularly expensive or rare, or can only be acquired through some kind of accomplishment like winning a tournament. These skins are considered the same as wearing Gucci, or a mark of ability. They signal that you are very good at this game and accomplished at it. You could think of them like medals on the chest of a military leader, or merit badges on the sash of a scout. Just the honor of being able to express to others these sorts of things is incredibly valuable.

In Belgium and The Netherlands, some of these virtual item systems have been outlawed or heavily regulated. Particularly, the concept of keys and loot crates. This is a way of selling digital assets through a psychological trick. Games occasionally give players loot crates. They promise that inside the crate is some kind of asset for the game that the player might want. The player can only open the crates with a key. The only way to get a key is to purchase one with real money. Keep in mind, this is a digital asset. There is no actual crate. There is no actual key. Inside the crate, there is no asset. There is literally nothing inside of it. It doesn't have an inside. It is a digital image of a crate. It is not a real crate.

By buying the key and using it on the crate, all you have done is triggered a random number generator to select a random asset for you. Because these assets are tradable and valuable, and because they are granted through a random number generation system using real money, some governments have interpreted this to be a form of gambling. These games are often very popular with children. Because in most places you have to be an adult to gamble, this creates a legal complication that hasn't been resolved yet. It is further made morally dubious on account that there is no regulation on it in the same way that any ordinary casino is regulated, and there is no way to calculate the odds in a normal way. You can calculate the odds of winning games of poker or craps. But the back-end math that creates this asset production machine is completely invisible and we are utterly reliant on the goodwill of the game studio.

The "loot" in these crates are essentially NFTs. A crate is an NFT that generates a different NFT when combined with a key NFT. If things are starting to sound weird to you, that is a great observation. It is going to get weird.

Chapter 7: How to Get Involved

The great success of companies like Apple and Microsoft are very easy to understand. They didn't need to have the most powerful computers, or the smartest engineers, or the newest ideas. What they did was make computers simple enough for normal people to use. They have gotten so good at this that most 65-year-old grandmothers have a supercomputer in their purse that they have no trouble operating. That computer is her iPhone or Android.

Cryptocurrencies started without developed marketplaces for trading online, without useful tools to measure fair market value and predict trends. It started out as very difficult to use, which was fine because the early adopters liked it enough despite this. But like Apple and Microsoft, developers and entrepreneurs made the frontend, the customer facing portion, much more approachable for ordinary people to dip their toes into it. There has never been a time easier to start than now. If you know how to buy things online, you know almost enough already to buy and sell NFTs.

How to Buy and Trade

Before you can buy an NFT, you need cryptocurrency to buy it with. Luckily, there are plenty of very well designed and trustworthy crypto exchanges. Finding them is as simple as a search on your desktop computer or your phone's app store. Binance, CoinbasePro, and Crypto.com are among the most popular services right now. We don't need to go into detail about how to use these apps, because they will do it for you when you download them and make an account.

These exchanges are the way most people trade in crypto assets. When you make an account, the service automatically generates a wallet for you, with the key in their custody. Keeping your money with this service requires trust because they have the keys to the wallet you are using on their service. If their security is breached, your wallet is breached. Experienced traders use these wallets for trading, but transfer their assets to another wallet that only they have the key to.

These services are very easy to use. They are designed to be as customer-friendly as they can, and they make entry into their market simple for inexperienced and curious people. If you find an exchange you like, it won't be challenging to make an account and start trading in cryptocurrency right away.

They will need you to link your account to some form of payment service so you can buy crypto with money, just like any online store, and this may require other identification such as a government-issued ID.

You will also want to make a wallet off of the exchange. The wallet on the exchange is in the custody of another company. Your crypto is only as secure as they are.

There are different kinds of wallets. There are digital wallets and physical wallets. A digital wallet is available to you online. A physical wallet stores the key on a physical device such as a cellphone, laptop computer, a thumb drive, or a specially designed ultra-secure device.

To get you started, we're going to begin by using a digital wallet. In the future, if you plan on investing heavily into crypto assets, you will want a physical device or a custodial service. For the time being, we're just playing around and learning, so that won't be necessary.

At the time of writing, the most popular services to create wallets are:

- MetaMask

- TrustWallet

- Dapper

- MyEtherWallet

When you are ready to make a physical wallet, the most popular options are:

- Ledger

- Trezor

These are considered the most popular at the time of publishing. This market is very dynamic, and there's no guarantee that they will stay at the top of the pack a year or two from now.

Once you've made a wallet, SAVE YOUR KEY. This cannot be emphasized enough. Write your key down on a physical sheet of paper. Hide it in a safe or bank safety deposit box, or any other very secure place. Save multiple copies and store them in multiple, very secure places. This key is all that is needed to access your wallet. If anyone else gets this key, they can walk right into your wallet and do what they like with whatever is inside.

There is no customer service rep you can call to get your assets back if they are stolen. There is no phone number to call or person you can show 3 forms of government-issued identification to get control of your wallet. Wallets aren't banks. No one can protect your wallet besides you, so make sure you keep it safe.

Once you have crypto to spend, you can search for an NFT exchange such as:

- OpenSea

- Rarible

- SuperRare

- Mintable

- Enjin

If you are interested in sports NFTs, you can try:

- NBATopShot

- Topps.com

Find what you like and buy something.

How to Make an NFT

Making an NFT is simpler than you might expect. You can make one right now if you like, but there is no promise that anyone will buy it. As the popularity grows, websites have to make their services more and more user friendly for casual users in order to grow their market share.

Step 1. Choose a Blockchain

There are countless blockchains to choose from other than Ethereum, and many of them are built off Ethereum. There's Binance's Smart Chain, EOS, Polkadot, Tezos, Cosmos, WAX, and others. Which one is right for you? That all depends on the market you are looking at. Ethereum is the obvious choice, especially for starters, as it is the biggest game in town. For your first time doing this, we're going to use Ethereum.

Step 2. Make a Wallet and Buy Some ETH

We covered this above, so if you already did it, move on to the next step.

Step 3. Use a Reliable Website to Create an NFT

OpenSea and Rarible are popular choices to make an NFT, because they make it so easy. Just go to their site and they'll walk you through their process.

Step 4. Pay the Gas Fee

When you are ready to make the NFT, you will need to pay ETH. The cost will depend on lots of factors, which we discussed earlier in the section on gas fees. If you don't have sufficient ETH to pay, you'll have to add funds to your wallet.

If these prices seem steep, you can wait to create it at a later time when prices are lower, but there is no guarantee that the prices will look more manageable soon. Like we talked about earlier, this market is very volatile and prices can move quickly and unexpectedly.

Step 5. Put Your NFT on a Marketplace

Whichever service you used to make your NFT also likely has a marketplace where you can sell it, if you wish to do so. There are a lot of marketplaces, some with their particular niche. A search with your browser of choice will give you some top results. Whatever you find first is what other people find first, too. If you want to sell, a search-engine-optimized market is a good place to go. If they got you there, they will bring a lot of other people there, too.

How to Watch the Market

Because the value of any crypto currency is tied to celebrities, in order to watch the market, you need to watch the celebrities. It is based on the respect and reputation of the creator more than anything else. Your most important tool is simply reading the news, particularly crypto news. Being aware of current events is more important than anything else.

If a celebrity athlete's career should have a major scandal, it's hard to predict how that could impact the card. If OJ Simson made an NFT in 1990, would the value of it be higher or lower now on account of his reputation? Both seem plausible. How about former NFL player Phillip Adams? He murdered an entire family. Would his NFT's price go up or down in that situation? We haven't seen this happen yet, so we can't know for certain. It's a fair bet that in the early moments of a scandal of that kind, the value would go down, as no one would be proud to own the NFT of a murderer. However, over the long run, when the emotions of the events have cooled down and the person becomes a fascination of true crime fans, the value could go up considerably. An NFT of Charles Manson's music would be considered repulsive in 1970, but it might be a very sought after collector's item in 2021.

An NFT sale could also be a signal of desperation. A comedian whose career is in decline might try to make an NFT to make a little bit of money. This could look like a money grab as their popularity is sunsetting. Even selling it at all might send that signal. Whoever buys it might find the value depreciates with the popularity of the person. How much would anyone pay for a Carlos Mencia token?

Because the tech is new, and there is so much innovation, strange projects will make big splashes. Value can also come from sheer novelty. CryptoPunks was an art project of 10,000 unique 8-bit images of heads. All of them were given out for free. Because they were the first images ever put on the blockchain, some are individually worth millions. The art isn't impressive at all. It's not about that. It's that they were the first. There will be other firsts. If you want to make money in this market, you have to be informed enough or lucky enough to get there before everyone else realizes it.

Sometimes the value of a thing isn't from who made it, but from who possessed it. A compass made by an anonymous Italian compass-maker in the 15th Century would be a very cool collector's item. But if that compass was owned by Christopher Columbus on his famous westward exploration, the value of it would be phenomenally higher. Who has owned this NFT? It could be valuable just because a famous person or people had it. If you remember all the way back to the start of this book, we talked about a hypothetical Anthony Kiedis t-shirt. An NFT that has passed through the possession of a famous person might get some of that fame rubbed onto them. An otherwise unremarkable NFT that was traded between several Hollywood actors might be very interesting for collectors, simply because they were once in their possession.

Chapter 8: The Future

The possibilities of what NFT smart contracts can look like are limited only to what a computer can do. This book can't be complete because the story of NFTs is only getting started. If you follow it to its logical conclusion, it starts to sound a lot like science fiction. Jules Verne's ideas about travel on Earth used to be fiction, too, until they were realized with actual science.

Implications of the New Tech

Smart contracts can also be used in the traditional stock market and financial trades without the need of a bank or any kind of professional trader. The trading of derivatives can be handled entirely through smart contracts, cutting out any kind of middlemen from the business. Smart contracts could handle complicated things like forwards and futures contracts. Smart contracts can handle bonds, loans, payables, and receivables. Ethereum could potentially remove any need for payment processors such as Stripe or PayPal.

Smart contracts could be used in tandem with copyright. The NFT could itself contain a legal contract giving ownership of the IP bundled inside of it. This means that if someone wants to stream a piece of music or sell rights to a TV car commercial, they have to negotiate that deal with the owners of the NFT. This could change everything.

In the same way that contracts are often built out of boilerplate clauses—lines of text that have proven themselves to be reliable under the scrutiny of courts—we can expect to see something similar for smart contracts. There are several popular websites where computer programmers and hackers share the source code of their projects in an open-source environment. Source code is the code that the programmers type in. If you have access to the source code, you can simply copy and paste that code into any project you are working on very easily, just like you could while writing a document using MS Word.

Over time, we can expect certain smart contracts to prove themselves to be reliable and become standard boilerplate code. We can likewise expect culture to develop around expectations about what goes into smart contracts. Even a layperson who is not trained in law understands the concept of a non-disclosure agreement, despite that being a legal concept. We can expect the same for lines of code. Digital instructions in smart contracts will also be as prevalent and easy to understand as non-disclosure agreements.

Every middleman industry that works with a product that can be digitized is very focused on crypto right now. This includes art galleries, record labels, film studios, banks, hedge funds, and everyone else. A lot of very important people could lose a lot or gain a lot depending on the choices they make right now.

A Dark Side

Not all of the implications of this tech are optimistic.

To use a grotesque example, consider Charles Manson's music. Besides being a cult leader and murderer, Manson was also a failed musician. His music was not considered valuable until he was famous for things less wholesome. If he had made an NFT before his cult members went on a murdering spree, his tokenized music would likely become instantly very sought after. Celebrities can make an NFT. Sometimes those celebrities are famous for the worst kind of reason. Perish the thought that a person would commit a heinous act for the express purpose of increasing the price of an NFT, but crazier things have happened.

Now consider this chilling idea: it is possible to create an NFT of revenge porn or child pornography and release it onto the blockchain. Only the person with the wallet can access it and whoever has that wallet is anonymous. There haven't been any major news stories about this happening yet, but it is inevitably going to be something society will have to reckon with. Remember: nothing on the chain can be removed. It is there forever. For all we know, there are already vast amounts of encrypted, illegal material being passed around through the planetary-wide distributed mining system right now.

Think of the Possibilities

Instead of an original copy being under the custody of a studio, a new song can be released and then purchased in pieces exactly like an IPO. We might expect some time in the future for Kanye West to make an announcement about a new song and then offer investors to jump in on it and buy up fractions of the rights to it, exactly like a corporation or a movie production. The investors would expect to make money off of these investments based on projections of dividends or royalties of the song's profits through streaming services in exactly the same way that a producer might invest in a movie and then expect a percentage return on that investment.

Opening up investments like this could mean that ordinary people have the opportunity to invest in media in a way that was previously only available to very moneyed and very influential people. What if there was a stock of "Imagine" by John Lennon? That would be a very expensive and valuable song, and you might only be able to hold 1/1000th of it as property, depending on your financial situation. Then, in this new digital era, perhaps anytime "Imagine" is played in a movie, played on the radio, played through Spotify, or purchased through Apple's iTunes, a tiny fraction of a penny would be deposited into your bank account from now into perpetuity. You might find the song to be a large initial investment, but it might pay off nicely in the future.

Don't be surprised if you see futures trading for things like John Lennon's "Imagine" in times to come as a way of hedging against risk in a larger hedge funds portfolio.

Because of the universality of NFTs and the impossibility to forge them, we might see NFTs used as a form of personal identification. Instead of purchasing a digital ticket, you might purchase that ticket as a form of NFT. Then that concert or sports game song has a diesel stub which might in itself become a collector's item. For example, if you had a digital stub for the last show performed by Willie Nelson, that stub might have a particular value on account of it being his last show. And in 20 years, you might find digital stuff that has some sentimental value to you and chase after it and buy it simply for that.

NFTs could be valuable simply as a means of pre-release for a new product. If several people were to invest in a big studio movie production, for example, their ownership of it through the portion of the NFTs might entitle them to witness an early release of the movie before anyone else had the opportunity. This itself could easily spike the price of the NFT before the movie came out. When certain very highly anticipated movies would be released, people would buy out the initial ticket sales instantly and show up to the movie that was built to air at exactly one second after their contract was released. People will pay a premium to be the first to see something like that. You can imagine the profit that Disney would make by selling tiny fractions of a property for a new Star Wars movie while offering a week's early access to it for anyone who buys into it. This has profitable implications, not just for movies, but for anything that can be transmitted digitally that would be of interest to people. A new book or a new album by a famous content creator could be extremely interesting for fans.

In the future, we might even expect hostile takeovers of intellectual property by consolidating shares of it under one person or corporation and getting controlling shares of it. This could be a strange future for anyone's rights.

We talked earlier about tokenized items in video games. Right now the company that makes and runs the game has all of the power over the make-believe items that they sell. In the future, we should expect to see a situation where the items have cross-platform compatibility. You might be able to plug an NFT into all types of things. You might be able to use that singularly-owned piece of art in your possession as a banner on Facebook. The contract built around that piece of art might say that you are the only person who can have that piece of art on Facebook. If Facebook gets involved, they could design a system so that art is authenticated and check ownership of that NFT. Counterfeits and copies might be impossible to upload as a banner onto Facebook. It becomes like your piece of art on your digital wall. You could plug this piece of art into video games and your character could have that graphic on their t-shirt. You would be the only person in the world in that video game with that t-shirt.

Imagine a future of blockchain journalism, where information can be leaked without the possibility of government censorship or the approval of tech giants for a platform.

Imagine NFTs with smart contracts that automatically generate other NFTs.

Imagine recursively self-altering NFTs, that create slightly different copies of themselves and then "burn" themselves by moving themselves into unknown wallets, creating an NFT that automatically evolves into new things forever.

Imagine sales of NFTs for charity, allowing the buyer to signal a devotion to an issue.

Possession is 90% of the law. Imagine automated return of ownership of NFTs if a portion of a smart contract is breached, seizing ownership, completely negating the need for laws to enforce contracts at all.

If you can imagine it, and a computer can do it, it's a possibility.

Distributed IP Going Forward

Rest assured that there are very inventive and creative people who will develop many applications for these digital objects over the coming years in ways that we can't anticipate.

Digital artist Krista Kim sold the first digital NFT house for half a million dollars. The house only exists as a 3D schematic on the internet. This house is part of what's called the "Metaverse," a persistent, shared virtual space. In English, the house is virtual reality real-estate. With virtual reality becoming more affordable and popular all the time, we should expect to see an entire parallel virtual economy emerging soon.

The sudden interest in NFTs has put a lot of energy into these virtual spaces through publicity and profit motive. If we are heading more and more into a world where the real and virtual overlap, a parallel virtual economy should soon be so integrated into our physical world that in the future the two will seem inseparable. The middle-point between VR and reality is called "augmented reality," where a headset overlaps virtual images on top of the real one. Could this include virtual fashion, where virtual clothes are rendered over a person when someone looks through the AR glasses? Maybe someday famous designers will make virtual clothes that aren't limited by natural constraints.

ETH 2.0

The next iteration and upgrade of the Ethereum network aims to solve three problems

Reduce Network Congestion. As Ethereum's popularity grows, the system slows down without more power.

Reduce Required Disk Space. The computer space necessary to run nodes on the network is higher and becoming less available to people, which makes the network less distributed, and more contained in the hands of a few, well-financed operations.

Reduce Energy Thirst. As the network grows, the amount of electricity used increases. This makes everything more expensive and more impactful on the environment.

The new Ethereum breaks up the enormous single chain into several smaller chains and randomly assigns validators. This way, each node only needs to handle one much smaller chain. Smaller chains mean fewer blocks, which means fewer blocks that need to be verified.

Ethereum currently works on a proof-of-work system, where miners are rewarded for the amount of computer power invested in maintaining the network. Because this is a competitive model, there is a lot of waste as many different computers compete to perform the same function, but only a few with powerful machines and a little bit of luck can get the reward.

The new proof-of-stake system allows users to buy into the mining game by "staking" their ETH 1.0, taking it out of circulation, and buying permission to mine for the network. Doing this moves people towards 2.0 but keeps ETH 1.0 value strong because miners need it to mine. With less computing power necessary, the network is much more efficient, requires less electricity and computer power, and spreads the work out between more machines.

There's Always More to Learn

This is a short book that is designed to help you understand what NFTs are, why they matter, and how to get involved if you are interested. There is a lot of information in this book to process, but there is so much more out there. If this is something that interests you, there is always more to learn, depending on how deep you want to get into the culture of the art scene, the technology, or the nature of the market.

Technology is always changing, growing, and becoming more friendly to ordinary people who don't have advanced degrees in computer science. If you want to invest in this market, this book should be the first thing you read, but it can't be the last thing you read.

Conclusion

Maybe you aren't convinced that this is going to change anything. Maybe this seems like a fad. That's possible. The evidence is mounting that this is going to become a major part of digital ownership in the future, but for the sake of argument, let's allow that this is just a fad.

Bell bottoms were just a fad and clothing manufacturers made a lot of money selling them for almost two decades. Beanie Babies were a fad, but the TY corporation that manufactured them made a tremendous amount of money on it. Meanwhile, the collectors wasted money gambling that the toys' value would appreciate and someday pay for their child's college.

If you see a gold rush, you don't necessarily run to the hills to dig up gold. It's easier, safer, and in the long run more profitable, to sell shovels and pans and pickaxes.

Whether or not this is a fad or a bubble that's going to burst, doesn't mean that it is something you should ignore or that it is something that you cannot profit from. At some level, even horses were just a trend. That trend became outdated when cars became available.

When you think about it another way, maybe the traditional banking system that we are living with right now is just a trend. Maybe the way we handle IP has been a fad. Maybe the institutions were just a trend that has been with us for thousands of years. Maybe that trend is finally coming to its terminus, just like horses, feudalism, cotton gins, and barrel-making.

To paraphrase Hemmingway from *The Sun Also Rises*, "You go broke gradually, then suddenly." Technology is the same way. NFTs are not new. They've been developing slowly for years. Right now is the sudden part. This is the moment where it seems fast, because most people never noticed the slow part happening. The technology has arrived into mainstream awareness. Whether you invest yourself in NFTs and crypto or not, you need to understand what is about to happen. Whether an NFT image of Barry Sanders is overvalued is the least interesting thing happening. This technology is about to change the world.

References

Authers, J. (2021, April 9). Bitcoin is Displacing Gold as an Inflation Hedge. *Bloomberg.com*. https://www.bloomberg.com/opinion/articl es/2021-04-09/bitcoin-is-displacing-gold-as-an-inflation-hedge

Bailey, J. (2021, March 16). *NFTs and copyright - plagiarism today*. Plagiarism Today. https://www.plagiarismtoday.com/2021/03 /16/nfts-and-copyright/

Beck, J. (2021, March 2). *Can NFTs crack royalties and give more value to artists?* ConsenSys. https://consensys.net/blog/blockchain-explained/can-nfts-crack-royalties-and-give-more-value-to-artists/

BP statistical review of world energy 2018, 67th
edition. (n.d.). In *BP* (p. 49). Retrieved May 25,
2021, from
https://www.bp.com/content/dam/bp/bus
iness-
sites/en/global/corporate/pdfs/energy-
economics/statistical-review/bp-stats-
review-2018-full-report.pdf

C, A. (2021, March 27). *What are NFT stocks? Your guide
to non-fungible tokens*. Www.nasdaq.com.
https://www.nasdaq.com/articles/what-are-
nft-stocks-your-guide-to-non-fungible-
tokens-2021-03-27

Cambridge bitcoin electricity consumption index (CBECI).
(2021). Cbeci.org. https://cbeci.org/faq/

Cillizza, C. (2021, January 29). *Analysis: 2 charts that show just how old this congress actually is.* CNN. https://www.cnn.com/2021/01/29/politics/congress-age/index.html

CNN, L. K. (2021, March 24). *World's first digital NFT house sells for $500,000.* CNN. https://edition.cnn.com/style/article/digital-nft-mars-house-scli-intl/index.html

Crypto scam, frozen assets and missing CEO lead to raids in turkey. (2021, April 23). The Daily Hodl. https://dailyhodl.com/2021/04/23/crypto-scam-frozen-assets-and-missing-ceo-lead-to-raids-in-turkey/

Dittmar, L., & Praktiknjo, A. (2019). Could bitcoin emissions push global warming above 2 °C? *Nature Climate Change*, *9*(9), 656–657. https://doi.org/10.1038/s41558-019-0534-5

Dockrill, P. (2016, June 29). *This 5,000-year-old artefact shows ancient workers were paid in beer*. ScienceAlert. https://www.sciencealert.com/this-5-000-year-old-clay-tablet-shows-ancient-mesopotamians-were-paid-for-work-in-beer

Entrepreneur en Español. (2021). *A Man Who Forgot His Bitcoin Password Could Lose $220 Million*. Www.msn.com. https://www.msn.com/en-us/money/other/a-man-who-forgot-his-bitcoin-password-could-lose-220-million/ar-BB1cL47x

Green innovation in bitcoin mining: Recycling ASIC heat. (2021, February 25). Braiins.com. https://braiins.com/blog/green-innovation-in-bitcoin-mining-recycling-asic-heat

Kau, A. (2021, May 21). *Elon musk takes dogecoin on a wild ride after he tweets 1950s song, netizens baffled*. Republic World. https://www.republicworld.com/technolog y-news/other-tech-news/elon-musk-takes-dogecoin-on-a-wild-ride-after-he-tweets-1950s-song-netizens-baffled.html

Ludwig Von Mises, & Bettina Bien Greaves. (2007). *Human action: The treatise on economics*. Liberty Fund, Cop. https://mises.org/library/human-action-0/html

Marco, P. (2017). Bitcoin-mining-btc-crypto-currency-2883884/. In *pixabay.com*. https://pixabay.com/illustrations/bitcoin-mining-btc-crypto-currency-2883884/

Mollen, F. (2021, April 21). *IBM is working to turn patents into nfts with the help of a "patent troll."* CryptoPotato. https://cryptopotato.com/ibm-turning-patents-nft/

Renewables increasingly beat even cheapest coal competitors on cost. (2021, June 2). /Newsroom/Pressreleases/2020/Jun/Renewables-Increasingly-Beat-Even-Cheapest-Coal-Competitors-On-Cost. https://www.irena.org/newsroom/pressreleases/2020/Jun/Renewables-Increasingly-Beat-Even-Cheapest-Coal-Competitors-on-Cost#:~:text=%E2%80%9CRenewable%20energy%20is%20increasingly%20the

Rowlatt, J. (2021, February 27). How Bitcoin's vast energy use could burst its bubble. *BBC News.* https://www.bbc.com/news/science-environment-56215787

Weston, M. (2019, September 2). *Manny pacquiao has launched his very own cryptocurrency.* Www.unilad.co.uk. https://www.unilad.co.uk/technology/many-pacquiao-has-launched-his-very-own-cryptocurrency/

Wintermeyer, L. (2021, March 10). *Bitcoin's energy consumption is A highly charged debate – who's right?* Forbes. https://www.forbes.com/sites/lawrencewintermeyer/2021/03/10/bitcoins-energy-consumption-is-a-highly-charged-debate--whos-right/?sh=5b3514bc7e78

Witkowski, W. (2020, December 22). *Videogames are a bigger industry than sports and movies combined, thanks to the pandemic.* MarketWatch. https://www.marketwatch.com/story/video games-are-a-bigger-industry-than-sports-and-movies-combined-thanks-to-the-pandemic-11608654990

www.438marketing.com, 438-. (2021, May 12). *What exactly is trash art? The beginnings of a crypto art movement.* NFTS.WTF. https://nfts.wtf/what-exactly-is-trash-art/

Made in United States
North Haven, CT
19 April 2022

18399121R00063